HENRI BERGSON:
THE PHILOSOPHY OF CHANGE

HENRI BERGSON

HENRI BERGSON:

THE PHILOSOPHY OF CHANGE

By H. WILDON CARR

KENNIKAT PRESS
Port Washington, N. Y./London

194
C23h

HENRI BERGSON

First published in 1912
Reissued in 1970 by Kennikat Press
Library of Congress Catalog Card No: 70-103174
SBN 8046-0811-3

Manufactured by Taylor Publishing Company   Dallas, Texas

PREFACE

MONSIEUR HENRI BERGSON, the philosopher whose teaching I have tried to present in brief in this little manual, is still in the full vigour of his life and thought. He is a philosopher who combines profound and original thinking with a wonderful talent for clear exposition. He is a Professor at the College of France, and a Member of the Institute. Although his writing and teaching is in the language of his country, we English may claim a special share in him so far as there is any nationality in philosophy. It is very largely by the direct study of the classical English philosophers that the particular direction of his thought has been determined. The influence of Herbert Spencer and of John Stuart Mill, and also of the older English philosophers, Locke, Berkeley, and Hume, is clearly manifest in his writings. It is particularly shown in his attitude toward physical science. His philosophy is not an attempt to depreciate science or to throw doubt on scientific method, but, on the contrary, its whole aim is to enhance the value of science by showing its true place and function in the greater reality of life.

The purpose that I have kept in view in the following pages is to give the reader not a complete epitome of the philosophy so much as a general survey of its

scope and method. If the reader is interested and
desires to become a student there is only one advice
that I can give him, and that is to read Monsieur
Bergson's books. If the problems they deal with
interest him, he will find no difficulty in understanding them, for the author's style is a model of lucidity.

During this present year (1911) Monsieur Bergson
has become personally known to large circles of
philosophical students in England. In May he delivered two lectures before the University of Oxford
on "The Perception of Change." (*La Perception du
Changement.* Oxford, The Clarendon Press.) He
delivered the Huxley Lecture at the University of
Birmingham on "Life and Consciousness," published in the *Hibbert Journal*, October 1911. He
also delivered four lectures before the University
of London on "The Nature of the Soul." These
have not yet been published. Quite recently also
his Essay *Le Rire*, written in 1901, has been translated into English. (*Laughter, an Essay on the
Meaning of the Comic.* Macmillan & Co.)

I am alone responsible for the plan and method
that I have chosen in presenting this philosophy,
but Monsieur Bergson has very kindly read the proofs,
and the title I have given to it, *The Philosophy of
Change*, was suggested by him.

H. WILDON CARR.

BURY, SUSSEX,
December 1911.

CONTENTS

HENRI BERGSON:
THE PHILOSOPHY OF CHANGE

CHAPTER I

PHILOSOPHY AND LIFE

THE philosophy of Bergson is contained in three principal works, produced at considerable intervals of time and independently of one another. All three are now available for English readers, having been recently translated under the supervision of the author. The first of these, *Time and Freewill*, appeared in 1888, the original title being *The Immediate Data of Consciousness;* the second, *Matter and Memory*, appeared in 1896; and the last and best known, *Creative Evolution*, in 1907. The distinctive principle of Bergson's philosophy was clearly set forth in the earliest of these books; the later ones have not modified nor developed it, but rather may be said to have applied it with increasing confidence and success. To expound that principle and explain its application to the various problems that have been brought to light in the long history of philosophy is the aim of this volume. The philosophy of Bergson is not a system. It is not an account of the ultimate nature of the universe, which claims to be a complete representation in knowledge of all reality,

and which appeals to us for acceptance on the ground
of its consistency and harmony. We shall see that
óne of its most important conclusions is that the
universe is not a completed system of reality, of
which it is only our knowledge that is imperfect,
but that the universe is itself becoming. Consequently the value of the philosophy and the conviction that it will bring to the mind will be seen to
depend ultimately not on the irrefutability of its
logic, but on the reality and significance of the simple
facts of consciousness to which it directs our
attention.

Great scientific discoveries are often so simple in
their origin that the greatest wonder about them is
that humanity has had to wait so long for them.
They seem to lie in the sudden consciousness of the
significance of some familiar fact, a significance never
suspected because the fact is so familiar. Newton
and the falling apple, Watt and the steaming kettle,
will occur at once as illustrations of a principle that
seems to apply to many discoveries that have had
far-reaching results in practice. The same thing is
no less remarkable in philosophy; the discoveries
that have determined its direction have been most
often due to attention to facts so simple, so common
and of such everyday occurrence, that their very
simplicity and familiarity has screened them from
observation. No better illustration of this could be
found than is offered in the philosophy of Berkeley.
The famous theory *esse* is *percipi*, to be is to be
perceived, rests on an observation so ordinary that
its very simplicity was the only reason that had

made it possible to ignore it. When Berkeley said that reality was perception, he was calling attention to the fact that we all mean by reality what we perceive, and not something or other which we never do and never can perceive, which is by its definition unperceivable. Another illustration is the well-known case of the philosopher Kant, to whom it occurred that the laws of nature might be explained as the forms which the mind itself imposes on our knowledge, a conception which threw a new light on philosophical problems comparable to the revolution in astronomy that followed the Copernican theory that the earth instead of being, as was supposed, the fixed centre of the universe, was itself a planet revolving round the sun.

Now the fact to which Bergson has called our attention, which forms the foundation of his theory and has given a new direction to philosophy, is a fact of this extremely simple nature. If it be significant, if it has the significance which Bergson claims for it, it is due entirely to its extreme simplicity and familiarity that it has till now escaped our notice. It is the observation of the simple fact that deeper than any intellectual bond which binds a conscious creature to the reality in which it lives and which it may come to know, there is a vital bond. Our knowledge rests on an intuition which is not, at least which is never purely, intellectual. This intuition is of the very essence of life, and the intellect is formed from it by life, or is one of the forms that life has given to it in order to direct the activity and serve the purpose of the living beings that are endowed with it. The fundamental character of Bergson's philosophy is therefore to emphasise the primary importance of the conception of life as giving the key to the nature of knowledge. To understand knowledge we must first grasp the meaning of life.

It is this that distinguishes the philosophy of Bergson from all the systems ancient and modern that have preceded it, and also from contemporaneous theories, intellectualist and pragmatist. The intellect has been formed to serve the purposes of the activity which we call life. Knowledge is for life, and not life for knowledge. The key to the explanation of the problem of reality and knowledge does not lie within us in the mind, as the idealist contends, nor without us in the world of things in space, as the realist contends, but in life. Bergson's philosophy is not a theory of life; such a description would be quite inadequate to it. It is founded on the simple fact, to which he has called our attention, but which is simple and obvious directly it is pointed out, that life is the reality for which knowledge is and for which nature receives the order that knowledge discovers. The main task of philosophy is to do what science cannot do, comprehend life. The impetus of life, the springing forward, pushing, insinuating, incessantly changing movement of life has evolved the intellect to know the inert world of matter, and has given to matter the appearance of a solid, timeless existence spread out in space. Reality is not solid matter, nor thinking mind, but living, creative evolution.

It seems as if a great movement were in progress, sweeping us along in its course. To exist is to be alive, to be borne along in the living stream, as it were on the breast of a wave. The actual present now in which all existence is gathered up is this movement accomplishing itself. The past is gathered into it, exists in it, is carried along in it, as it presses forward into the future, which is continually and without intermission becoming actual. This reality is life. It is an unceasing becoming, which preserves the past and creates the future. The solid things which seem to abide and endure, which seem to resist this flowing, which seem more real than the flowing, are periods, cuts across the flowing, views that our mind takes of the living reality of which it is a part, in which it lives and moves, views of the reality prescribed and limited by the needs of its particular activity. This is the image of reality that is presented to us in Bergson's philosophy.

There is one difficulty that will at once present itself in the very attempt to understand an image of this kind. How can there be a pure movement, a pure change, a pure becoming ? There must be some object, some thing which moves, changes or becomes, and this thing must be supposed to be resting when it is not moving, to remain the same when it is not changing or becoming something else. This thing must be more real than its movement, which is only its change of place, or than its becoming, which is only its change of form. How is it possible to imagine that movement and becoming are alone reality, that they can subsist by themselves, and that the things that move and change are not prior to but productions of the movement or change ? It is a difficulty that goes to the very heart of the problem of philosophy. It is not the ordinary difficulty of realism and idealism, it is not the question of the nature of real existence whether it is physical or mental. It applies with equal force whatever we conceive the nature of a thing to be, whether thoughts are things or only about things, whether things exist only in the mind, or whether they exist independently and impress the mind. Whatever they are, it is things that move and change and become, and the movement and change and becoming presuppose that there are things.

So natural to us does this view of the reality of things seem, so consistent is it with our ordinary experience and with the teachings of science, that we are not usually aware that there is any difficulty in thinking of reality in this way. But there is a difficulty, which as soon as we understand it is more formidable and startling even than the seeming paradox that reality is a flowing. This is that our ordinary idea that the reality of things consists in their being solid objects in space, the idea that underlies the whole of physical science, involves the conception of an unreal time. Time as science conceives it does not form part of the reality of material things. When we perceive any ordinary unorganised material thing—water, air, a crystal, a metal—we do not think that time has anything to do with its reality, because whatever happens to it, it remains substantially the same. If water is separated into its component gases, it takes time to do it, but the reality is not altered, the gases are there, and can be re-combined into the water. We cannot, of course, imagine things without time, but the reason of this seems to be that imagination requires time, and not that time is necessary in order that things should exist. Time is a mode of existence, and it is only in this mode, that is, as states succeeding each other, that things are known, but the things exist independently of the succession of their states. A simple consideration will prove this. Suppose the rapidity of time to be double what it is, would it make any difference to the existence of material things ? Absolutely none. Indeed if we imagine the rapidity of the succession of states increased infinitely, even if we imagine the whole of the succession displayed simultaneously to an infinite intelligence, the reality of things will remain exactly what we now think it to be. There is no absolute material standard by which we measure time flow. Every standard of time measurement, such as the rotation of the earth on its axis, the revolution of the earth round the sun, or the swing of a pendulum, is relative. If all time relations remained constant to one another, a change in the actual rate of flow would make no difference to real things. Such a change is quite conceivable, but for the reality that is the subject-matter of science it is quite indifferent.

When we consider a living being, however, we find that time is the very essence of its life, the whole meaning of its reality. In life we meet with a real duration, a duration that is absolute. There is, it is true, for living creatures a time duration that is measured by the same relative standards by which we measure the succession of the states of material things. It is this unreal time that we have in mind when we speak of our fleeting existence and think of the things that outlast us; it gives meaning to such expressions as eternal youth. Life seems made up of definite states—infancy, childhood, adolescence, maturity, old age—which we pass through, and which we imagine have a period of stability and then change. But the change is continuous throughout each state, and the states are a merely external view of life. It is our body which enables us to take this view. Our body is an object in space, and we consequently regard it in this external way. But life itself, when we view it from within, from the privileged position that we occupy towards it by reason of our identity with it, is not indifferent to time. Our life as actual experience, as the inmost reality of which we are most sure, which we know as it exists, is time itself. Life is a flowing, a real becoming, a change that is a continuous undivided movement. A thing that lives is a thing that endures not by remaining the same, but by changing unceasingly. All consciousness is time existence, and a conscious state is not a state that endures without changing, it is a change without ceasing; when change ceases it ceases, it is itself nothing but change.

There are therefore two ways in which we may think of time, one in which it makes no difference to reality, and the other in which it is the reality. Just as we think that things lie outside one another in space, so we think that their states succeed one another in time. Time in this meaning takes the form of space; it can only be represented by us as a line, and a line is a figure in space. Without the idea of space we should be unable to represent the succession of states of things. When we think of these successive states we imagine them spread out in a continuous line, precisely as we imagine real things to be at any moment all spread out in space. But this is not true duration. Our life is true duration. It is a time flow that is not measured by some standard in relation to which it may be faster or slower. It is itself absolute, a flowing that never ceases, never repeats itself, an always present, changing, becoming, now.

The distinction between a time that is a symbol of space and a time that is a true duration is therefore fundamental. We may mean either of two different things when we ask, what is reality ? We may mean what is it that endures without changing ? Or we may mean, what is it that endures by changing ? The difference between the two meanings is the difference between a material thing and a living thing; to the one time does nothing and therefore is nothing, to the other time is everything. And so the question arises, is the reality that is behind all appearances like a material thing that does not change ? Or is it like a living thing whose whole existence is time ? The answer that philosophy must give is that time is real, the stuff of which things are made. Physical science is a view of this reality, a limited view, and the positive proof of it is that it cannot comprehend life. Life is not a thing nor the state of a thing. It is this limitation of physical science, its inability to understand life, that reveals to us the true sphere and the special task of philosophy. Physical science deals with the stable and unchanging, philosophy deals with life.

CHAPTER II

INTELLECT AND MATTER

I HAVE said that the philosophy of Bergson rests on the observation of a very simple fact. This simple fact is that true duration is known to us by a direct inner perceiving, an intuition, and not by an intellectual act such as that by which we perceive the objects around us and the laws of their successive states. And the true duration which we know when we have this intuition is life. There is therefore possible to us a direct answer to the question, to answer which is the problem of philosophy. What is reality ? We can answer, reality is life. And the answer is final, because we are not appealing to a concept of the understanding that demands further explanation. Life is not a thing nor the state of a thing. It is true that we can only express it in the form of a judgment. But what we affirm in that judgment is not a *that* of which we are still driven to ask *what*, it is not a content that we distinguish from existence, and therefore does not lead to the endless inquiry that baffles the intellectualist attempt to solve the problem. Life is not known as something presented to the mind, but immediately in the living consciousness of living.

Intuition in the sense in which this philosophy

affirms it has nóthing either mystical or even mysterious about it. It is not the special endowment of certain highly-gifted minds, enabling them to see what is hidden from ordinary intelligence. It is a power of knowledge that we may imagine to exist in everything that lives, even in plants, for it is simple consciousness of life. I do not of course mean that there is any ground to suppose that it exists actually in this wide extension, or indeed that it necessarily exists anywhere, but I do mean that it is so identical with life itself, that wherever there is life there might also be that consciousness of living that is intuition. But simple as this principle is, and universal as its potentiality may seem to be, it is in fact only at rare moments and by very concentrated attention that we may become able to possess this knowledge which is in very truth identical with being.

What then is the intellect ? It is to the mind what the eye or the ear is to the body. Just as in the course of evolution the body has become endowed with certain special sense organs which enable it to receive the revelation of the reality without, and at the same time limit the extent and the form of that revelation, so the intellect is a special adaptation of the mind which enables the being endowed with it to view the reality outside it, but which at the same time limits both the extent and the character of the view the mind takes. When we consider a special organ like the eye, we can see that its usefulness to the creature it serves depends quite as much on what it excludes as on what it admits. If the eye could take in the whole of visible reality it would be useless. It is because it limits the amount of light it admits, and narrows the range of visible things, that it serves the life purpose. The intellect appears to have been formed by the evolution of life in the same way and for a like purpose. It has been formed by a narrowing, a shrinking, a condensation of consciousness. It reveals its origin in the fringe which still surrounds it as a kind of nebulosity surrounding a luminous centre. And what is the purpose that the intellect serves ? It gives us views of reality. It cuts out in the flow the lines along which our activity moves. It delimits reality. It traces the lines of our interest. It selects. Just as the events which the historian chronicles are marked out by the guiding influence of some special interest, so the intellect follows the lines of interest of the activity it serves. Things, solid inert unchanging matter, constant laws by which things act and react on one another, are views of reality that the intellect is formed to take, limitations which by narrowing knowledge to the form that is useful serves the living purpose which has evolved it, and for which knowledge exists. The intellect views the reality as solid things because that view serves our ends. It is a real world that the intellect reveals to us, a reality that is not relative to our understanding, nor produced by our understanding; it is reality itself, but it is limited. The outlines of things, the grouping and arrangement of phenomena, are the modes of our apprehension, the lines that our interest traces. There is no formless reality, but also no form of reality is absolute. With other interests we should trace other lines, and we might have other modes of apprehension.

The intellect is cinematographical. This description is perhaps the happiest of any of the images that Bergson has used to illustrate his theory. The cinematograph takes views of a moving scene; each view represents a fixed position, and when the views are arranged side by side on the film and passed across the screen in rapid succession they present to us a moving picture. The views as they lie before us on the ribbon, as we look at them in passing from one to the next, do not give us this picture; to have the picture we must restore the movement, and this the cinematograph does. The fixed things that seem to us to lie side by side of one another at every moment in space are views that the intellect takes. These views seem to us to form the movement by their succession, the replacement of one by another seems to be the change, but the reality is the movement; it is a continuous change, not a succession of states, and the fixed things are views of it. These views are the physical objects that science deals with, and the method of science is cinematographical; change for it is nothing but the succession of fixed states. But a movement is indivisible, a change is indivisible, the divisions that we make in it, the immobilities that seem to compose it, are not divisions, but views of it. Nothing is immobile. Immobility is purely an appearance.

This perception that a movement is indivisible is the key to the solution of many problems insoluble without it. There is, for example, a self-contradiction in the ordinary idea which we have of motion, which is well illustrated in the famous paradoxes of the Greek philosopher Zeno of Elea. Motion, he declared, is impossible, for consider the flying arrow; to say that it moves is to say that it is in two places at the same time, but at every moment everything is at rest in one place, and if the arrow is motionless at every moment of its flight, then it is always motionless. We can now see the solution of this problem. The flight of the arrow is an indivisible movement. We, looking at the course of the flight, represent it as a line along which we can make as many divisions as we choose. We say that the arrow passed over that course and that it might have stopped at any point. And that is so. But the divisions in the course are not divisions in the movement. If the arrow had stopped at any point of its course, its flight, the movement, would have ended; the subsequent flight would not have been a continuation of the movement, but a new movement. When the movement is effected we look back on the course and represent it as a line in space. A line is unmovable, space of which it is a figure is the very idea of immobility, and a line is divisible without limit, but movement is indivisibility itself. A line therefore cannot correspond with a movement; it is our representation of the movement, our view of it, an appearance only. Another famous argument of Zeno may be solved by the same perception that a movement is indivisible, the problem of Achilles and the tortoise. Achilles, it is argued, can never over-

take the tortoise, because while his first step brings
him to the place where the tortoise is, the tortoise
has moved on, and while he makes the new step to
reach the new place, the tortoise has again moved
on, so that Achilles for ever finds that he has still a
step to take. The problem is quite insoluble. if a
movement is divisible as a line is, but the difficulty
vanishes with the perception that a movement is
indivisible. The steps of Achilles and the steps of
the tortoise are each indivisible, each a simple continuity from beginning to end, and there is consequently no contradiction in supposing that the steps
of Achilles bring him past the tortoise. The contradiction lies altogether in regarding a step as made
up of parts like the separate views on the cinematograph film, in thinking that the parts exist
independently in the step, and that the combination
of the parts produces the step, and in failing to see
that the step is an indivisible movement, that the
parts into which we seem able to divide it are only
views that we take of it. Another of the paradoxes
of Zeno illustrates in an even more striking manner
the contradiction which follows the attempt to conceive movement by representing it as a spatial
figure. It is the argument known as the Stadium.
It is not so familiar as the others, because the paradox
is not so immediately self-evident as in the illustration of the arrow and of Achilles and the tortoise.
Two processions of figures moving round the stadium
in opposite directions pass in mid course a row of
similar figures at rest. The speed of the moving
figures, said Zeno, is twice that which it is, for

when the three rows of figures are in line with one
another, that is, at the moment when each procession is passing the other procession and the inter-
vening row, the space occupied by each of the three
rows is exactly equal, yet the velocity of each moving
row is to one another twice what it is to the inter-
vening row. And the two velocities are not relative,
they are absolute, because space does not move. We
have therefore to admit that a body moves at two
velocities at the same time, one of which is twice
that of the other. It may seem that this is a trans-
parent and very simple fallacy. It may even be
denied that there is the appearance of contradiction,
for if we have two reverse movements at equal
velocities, the velocity of each to the other is the
sum of the two and double what each is by itself.
Very true, but why ? Because when we make this
answer, which seems so obvious, we are comparing
movement with movement, treating it as indivisible,
just as we found we had to do with the steps of
Achilles and the tortoise. Make the movement
correspond with the space traversed, and you find
that the same movement measured by two exactly
equal spaces has passed at two different velocities ;
you find that you are making the contradictory
assertion that every movement is faster than it is.
The solution is plain and self-evident enough when
you perceive that movement is not divisible, that
you cannot decompose it into small movements
strung together, or joined together, as you can
decompose a line into smaller lengths. Divide a
line into as many lengths as you will, the sum of

those lengths is the line, but to divide a movement
is impossible; its divisions are not points, but stops.
We may suppose an infinity of points in a line, but
to suppose even one stop in a movement is contradictory; a stop is not part of a movement, but the
negation of movement.

We have seen that, like the cinematograph, the
intellect takes views across a moving scene, and
these views are the things that present themselves
to us as solid objects spread out in space, space that
is unmovable, the reality in which things move.
To grasp the reality, we have said, it is necessary to
restore the movement as the cinematograph does.
The movement is life. What, then, is matter ? What
is that inert something which is essentially opposed
to life, and which seems necessary to the existence
of life ? When we say of our own existence that it
is essentially our life, we are distinguishing life from
the material body which appears to serve as its
substratum or medium. And when we say of the
all-inclusive reality of which our individual lives are
but a partial manifestation, when we say of the
universe itself that it lives, it seems that we must
distinguish within the universe the life of it from the
inert, lifeless material, the dead matter in which that
life is supported and manifested. What is this dead
matter, and how does it come to exist ? Reality is a
flowing. This does not mean that everything moves,
changes, and becomes; science and common experience tell us that. It means that movement, change,
becoming is everything that there is, there is nothing
else. There are no things that move and change and

become; everything is movement, is change, is becoming. You have not grasped the central idea of
this philosophy, you have not perceived true duration, you have not got the true idea of change and
becoming until you perceive duration, change, movement, becoming, to be reality, the whole and only
reality. Inert matter filling space, space that underlies matter as a pure immobility, do not exist. Movement exists, immobility does not. Now even
physical science, bound as it seems to be to the
assertion of a fixed material reality, is being driven
to the same conclusion. In the new theory of matter
the old conception of an elemental solid base for the
atom has entirely disappeared, and the atom is now
held to be composed of magnetic forces, ions and
corpuscles, in incessant movement, a balance of
actions and reactions no longer considered indestructible. In fact, if the movement ceases the atom
no longer exists, there is nothing left. Again, the
most instantaneous flash of light that we can be
aware of contains, so science tells us, millions of
millions of æther waves. Light is nothing but
movement. In fact for science all things are in
movement. And also there is something that is
absolute in time duration even for physical science,
for though time does not enter into the reality of
things as science conceives them, yet a certain
length of time duration is a necessary condition of
every change in the state of things. A lump of
sugar does not instantaneously dissolve in a glass
of water; when all other actual conditions of dis-
solution are present, a certain time must elapse.

Still for science matter is the reality, time is only a condition. What then for philosophy which perceives that time is reality, the stuff out of which matter is formed, is this matter ? What is this inert something that seems to resist the pushing, forward moving life, which seems to fall back, to obstruct the living movement, which even when it serves life seems essentially opposed to it ? Inert matter, immobility, is purely an appearance, it is composed of two movements. It is the relation of our movement to other movements. When we are in a train the landscape seems to stream past us, the nearer objects at a greater speed than the more distant. When we pass another train going in the same direction but at a slower speed, it seems to us to be moving in the reverse direction. If the speed is the same as ours, it seems not to be moving at all. And if it is travelling in the reverse direction, it seems to be moving at twice the speed that it is really moving at. Imagine, then, life as a vast movement in being; if our particular interest draws us to attend to the direction in which part of the movement is advancing, it may seem to us that the rest of the movement is retarding the advance or even streaming backwards. So we, alive in this great living, borne along as part of this true life, view the movement around us and see it as dead matter opposed to the very movement of which it is itself only an individual view.

CHAPTER III

INSTINCT AND INTELLIGENCE

IF the theory of the intellect sketched in the last chapter is true, we shall expect to find that the intellect is not the only means by which it is possible to apprehend reality. It seems as we look back on the past from our own human standpoint, and try to read by the light of biological and geological science the long history of the evolution of life, and particularly of the human race, that this wonderful intellectual power that we possess, and that gives us such command in our world, has been a very slowly perfected acquisition. Our whole bodily organisation has been moulded to use it, and it has been mutually adapted to our organism, to serve its needs and to direct its activity. It is the very essence of our life, all that life means or can mean to us, but it is essentially an adaptation of life. The intellect is what gives to the world the aspect it bears to us. It gives us views of reality, views that are limitations of our apprehension, and that we mistake for limitations of reality. We have said that we have the power of apprehending reality without the limitations that the intellect imposes, that in the intuition of life we see reality as it is. This intuition is the consciousness of life that we have in living. It is not another and different power, it is not an endowment of the mind or a faculty. Intuition is not a kind of mental organ as the eye or the ear is a bodily organ, something that we possess side by side with the intellect. It exists for us because consciousness is wider than intellect, because consciousness is identical with life. In knowing life we are living, and in living we know life. In the widest signification of the terms, life and consciousness are identical. It is this wider consciousness that has become for us narrowed and specialised in the intellect, but the intellect reveals its origin by the wider sense of consciousness which surrounds it like a penumbra. It is this wider consciousness that enables us to have the direct vision that we have called the intuition of life. But it is only life that this intuition reveals, and that because life and consciousness are one. We have not therefore two faculties, one intellectual and one intuitional, side by side; there is not, that is to say, both an intellectual and an intuitional view of reality; all our views of reality are intellectual, but the intellect is formed out of the consciousness that is identical with life, and in living we do directly know life. This is the simple fact that, as I have endeavoured to show, is neither mystical nor mysterious.

But if the intellect is a special adaptation of the consciousness which is life, we shall naturally conclude that it might have been other than it is, and that it is possible that with other directions of the evolutionary activity other adaptations with other limitations would have been produced. And this is what we find. There is one other mode of mental activity, instinct, that we find some traces of in our own consciousness, but that has received striking and astonishing development along other lines of evolution than that which has culminated in man. Along the line of the vertebrates that has ended in ourselves it seems as though there must have been at first a hesitation as to which mode, instinct, or intelligence was to prevail. So much is this so, so slight seem the indications of intelligent, so universal the indications of instinctive behaviour in the forms of animal life below the human, and so sudden seems the development of perfect intelligence in man, that the opinion has been generally, and is still widely, held that intelligence is a development of instinct, and that instinct is nothing but a primitive form of intelligence. But when we study the behaviour of insects we find instinct brought to a perfection that rivals, or even surpasses, the intelligence of man. Especially is this so in the ants and the bees. These creatures represent the culminating point of a progressive evolution of instinct. Their marvellous actions can only be explained by supposing that instinct is a quite different and, in a certain manner, opposite mode of mental activity to that by which we apprehend reality. They are opposite modes, because though they may exist together, and though the one may at any time give place to the other, yet so far as the essential nature of each is concerned the one seems to block the other. We never find in any creature the simultaneous perfecting of the two modes. In man, where intelligence is

C

supreme, instinct is practically lost as a guiding and directing activity. We find traces of it in the behaviour of infants and children and in natural dispositions, but the very word instinctive has come to denote the opposite of rational action and not the basis of it. On the other hand, in the insect communities of bees and ants instinct is so perfect and so supreme as the guiding principle of their activity, that intelligence, if they possess it, must lie on a lower plane, or be manifested only in emergencies where instinct fails.

The actions that we call instinctive in man are those that we seem to carry out by a natural disposition without reflection, without interposing the perception of the relations or of the meaning of the actions, without the presentation to the mind of an end to be attained. They are not simple reactions to a stimulus, such as the vital functions of respiration, circulation, and the like; they are actions that imply awareness and conscious purpose, but they are direct spontaneous actions evoked by the presence of physical objects or of emotions. Such actions as the raising of the arm to ward off a blow, as flight when we feel the emotion of fear, the actions that are prompted by the emotions of love, pity, indignation, and the like, we call instincts. Instinct as prompting to these actions is knowledge that we seem to possess naturally, and without needing to be taught by experience. Many actions that are in their origin intelligent we call instinctive by analogy when they have become habitual. It is in the observation of the actions of infants and children that we distinguish most clearly the knowledge we call instinctive from that which we call intelligent. The infant's first cry is purely reflex, the vital action of drawing the air into the lungs ; sucking, at least in its earliest exercise, probably is so too; but the movements towards the mother's breast, the attraction to certain objects and repulsion from others we call instinctive, because these are evidence of a natural knowledge, a knowledge not acquired by experience, of a distinct and separate object. The child's first efforts to stand and walk are instincts, but the almost equally universal struggle of the child that can walk to get out of the perambulator and push it is intelligent, it is the result of observation and attention and desire to imitate. From infancy onwards the whole of our mental life is so predominantly intelligent that it is with the greatest difficulty that we are able to distinguish and recognise instincts. In man instinct does not develop but gives way to intelligence, as though the two modes were incompatible and intelligence to exist must supersede instinct.

It is when we observe the actions of insects, particularly the actions of the higher insects, that we see the most perfect examples of instinct, and become aware that it is a mental activity totally different from intelligence. It is true that the bees and ants among which we find this activity in its most marvellous manifestation present to us a type of bodily organisation so entirely different from our own, that comparison seems almost fantastic. The mentality of a dog or a horse, or even that of a bird or a reptile or a fish, seems possible to understand, because the bodily organisation of these animals and the anatomical structure of the centralised nervous system that serves their organism are constructed on an exactly similar plan to our own. But how widely different the whole plan of the invertebrate anatomy ! Is there any basis on which we can compare the mentality of such unlike creatures with our own ? Is it not mere picture thinking to try to interpret their actions by our knowledge of our own mental processes ? And it seems to many students of animal psychology that to attempt to understand instinct as a mental reality by the observation of insect life is entirely vain. But wide as the difference is between these small creatures and ourselves, we are in the presence of distinct self-centred individuals as vitally interested in pursuing their purposes as we are ourselves. They are organised to apprehend reality by special senses, and they have a nervous system of the same type as our own, the type that biologists call sensori-motor. Clearly they feel, whether or not their feelings have the same quality as ours, and their feelings lead to movements.

When now we study the life activities of these creatures, what do we find ? If we watch a swarm of bees in an observation hive we may see the perfect insects emerging from the cells in which they have been formed. We may neglect the early stages of their life, the egg and the pupa, as we are not now concerned with biology but only with psychology. From the very moment of their birth they know perfectly the work they have to do. They do not begin with vain efforts and with experience gain confidence and skill. They are not taught by older bees. They do not seem to be recognised by their fellows nor to recognise them, but immediately join in the common work, giving their service just where it is required, gathering honey and pollen, storing it in cells, tending brood, ventilating the hive or guarding the queen. They do this work, and they discern the special work required of them, as well on their first emergence into the community as when they are old and worn-out members of it. It may of course be that the actual bonds of unity are not perceived by us, that the true individual is the hive and not the separate insects that compose it, that the relation of the individual bees to the hive is more of the nature of the relation of the separate cells of the body to the organism than that of the relation of persons in a community. But whether that be so or not, we have before us individual creatures who lead individual lives, and who possess a knowledge which, unlike ours, is perfect from the first, and not, like ours, dependent on experience. Innumerable cases of instinct will also occur to every one in which a highly complicated action is performed once and once only in the insect's life, in which the creature cannot be aware of the effect or purpose of the action it performs judged by the result as we know it. The Yucca moth, for example, lays its eggs on the ovules of the Yucca flower, and then carefully fertilises the pistil with pollen, the result being that the seeds form the food of the larva, but the eggs are

laid on fewer ovules than are fertilised, so that pro-
vision is thereby made that all the seeds shall not
be destroyed by the larva. The Yucca plant is
dependent on this moth for the fertilisation of its
flowers, and the single performance of this act practically accomplishes the life purpose of the moth.
The insect acts as though it knew that its larva
would require ripe seed of the Yucca, as though it
knew that this could only be obtained by fertilisation,
as though it knew that ripe seed is also necessary for
the continuance of the existence of Yucca plants, and
therefore for the activity of Yucca moths; and yet
it is manifestly impossible that it can possess this
knowledge, much less acquire it in any intelligible
sense of the word knowledge. Why, then, do we
call instinct knowledge? What is there in a case
of this kind more than an unusually interesting
example of a biological fact of mutual adaptation,
to be explained by a biological theory such as that
of natural selection? The moth no more knows all
these things to which its action is directed than the
ivy knows that it is clinging to a wall, or the hop
plant that it must wind round a pole. Do we not
mean by instinct a vital force of adaptation that is
not knowledge at all in any usual sense of the term?
Do we not, in fact, speak of the instincts of plants?
Are not instincts the natural affinities of organisms
mutually dependent on one another, and the actions
that mutual dependence involves? Undoubtedly,
but there is also a problem of knowledge, a problem
that is psychological and philosophical, distinct from
every physical and biological fact. These creatures,

whose structure is so unlike our own, whose life activity is so different in its direction, nevertheless possess some kind of mentality. They are conscious of a world in which their activity is exercised. They receive revelations of reality through special sense-organs just as we do, and they guide their activity by the revelations so received. Sense impressions make them aware, awareness produces movements, and we judge of the nature of the awareness by the movements. These actions prove to us that instinct is a psychical activity, different in its mode of working and in the nature of its mentality from intelligence, and that there is an essential difference in the kind of knowledge that is accessible to it.

There is one very marked difference between instinctive and intelligent action in the consciousness or unconsciousness with which it is performed. We use the word consciousness in this connection in a very special sense. In its widest and most general meaning consciousness is almost synonymous with life. Everything that has the vital power of responding to a stimulus we call conscious as distinct from inert dead material which has no such power. In this sense consciousness means the possibility of any awareness whatever. But we also use the words conscious and unconscious in a special sense. We say that a man is unconscious when he is asleep, or under an anæsthetic; a man walking in his sleep may be carrying out very complicated actions, actions that show that he is in some sense aware of the surroundings in which he is moving, but we say that he is unconscious of what he is doing. In this sense of the word we do not mean by unconsciousness a complete absence of consciousness, as when we say that a stone is unconscious; we mean that the consciousness which is present is blocked or hindered from being effective. Rouse a man from his sleep, startle the sleep-walker in what he is doing, remove the anæsthetic that is being administered to the suffering patient, and consciousness returns. Many of our habitual actions, in fact by far the greater number of them, are unconsciously performed. Consciousness means an active attention to the work that is being performed, and this active attention seems to be a necessary condition of intelligence. Now instinct seems to us to be entirely unconscious. Bees constructing their cells seem to us to be following an impulse that is a natural disposition, and to be altogether unconscious of the design they are following or of the purpose or plan of the work they are doing. Men building a house, on the other hand, seem to be necessarily conscious of the plan they have to follow and of the purpose that their work has to fulfil. And this seems to us the main, if not the only, difference between instinct and intelligence. It seems to us that bees are really intelligent, that their instincts have arisen in an active attention to an intelligent purpose, but that their actions have become by long-continued habit and inherited characteristics automatic and unconscious. What seems to us extraordinary is that with such perfected natural knowledge they do not now use the intelligence which we think must have been at the origin of this knowledge. Perhaps we account for it by imagining that they still do actively use their intelligence, but that it is manifested on a plane that we are, possibly by a natural disability, incapacitated from observing, in like manner as we might imagine that higher beings observing us might think that our actions were automatic and fail to perceive the practically invisible plane on which our intellect works. Or we may even hold that there are instances of individual behaviour, or even of general behaviour, in insects which prove this active intelligence. We think then of instinct and intelligence as being in their origin and nature identically the same, differing only in the consciousness or unconsciousness that characterises the activity. Instinct is intelligence become automatic, and intelligence is always tending to become instinct. The special development and perfection of particular instincts we attribute to the aid of a special organic evolution. But in this view we fail to take account of the profound difference in the nature of the knowledge itself that instinct possesses and that which intelligence gives us. It is this difference in the nature of the knowledge that is the reason why instinctive knowledge is mainly unconscious and intelligence essentially conscious.

Instinctive action is immediate and direct, the apprehension of the object is followed by the appropriate action without any interval of hesitation, without any time for deliberation and choice. Intelligence, on the other hand, is just this hesitation, deliberation, and choice. Between the apprehension and the action there intervenes the representation of the action as an act carried out. It is the presence of this picture, the comparison of the various courses of action represented in idea before the action is started, that constitutes intelligence. The intellect gives us the power to choose, a power dependent on the ideal representation of the action before it is acted. When, therefore, in nearly all instinctive action, and in intelligent action that has become habitual, or when for any cause the action takes place without the intervention of representation, the action is unconscious. The very expressions we use, such as, to act without thinking, to act instinctively, imply that the action blocks out or hinders the representation. Instinct is immediate knowledge, knowledge such as intuition gives us, and being continued in the action, is therefore unconscious; intelligence represents the action in idea before it acts, hesitates and deliberates, and is therefore conscious.

This brings us to the really essential distinction between instinct and intelligence, the actual distinction in the kind of knowledge that each is fitted to give us. Intelligence is the knowledge of the relations of things. We may know a thing by instinct more perfectly than we can ever know it by intelligence, but it is intelligence alone that gives us the knowledge of relations, and it is this knowledge that gives us command over the wide field of activity that we possess. Intelligence is the power of asking questions. The number of things of vital consequence to it that a human child actually knows is very small compared with the knowledge the young of many of the lower animals have, but the child has a power that no lower animal has in anything like the same degree, the power of understanding the relation of a predicate to a subject, the power of using verbs. It can deduce conclusions and make inferences, and in this its intelligence lies. But that which chiefly marks the high intellectual attainment of man, that which is the most simple and concrete manifestation of his superiority, is the ability to make and use tools. It is here that we see the wide range of intelligence and the nature of the knowledge that it gives, as compared with the narrow range of instinct, perfect as its knowledge is. The tool that an insect uses is part of its bodily structure; it is far more perfect for its purpose than any human tool, and with it is always the special instinct that prompts the animal to use it. It has perfect skill, but restricted to a very narrow range. The tool that a man uses is made of any material; it is very imperfect compared to the natural tool, but it is capable of infinite variation and adaptability. The sharpened flint, the stone tied to a stick to make a hammer, such are the simple primitive indications of pure intelligence, and the progress of the human race is marked by the enormous extension of this simple power of using dead material to fashion more and more perfect tools. The detachability and adaptability of the material we use is derived from this power we have to know relations. It is further illustrated in our language, which more than anything else is recognised as a mark of intelligence and which serves the intelligence that it is the sign of. Language is communication by signs, signs that are entirely detached from and different from the thing signified. Insects and lower animals doubtless communicate with their fellows, but we cannot imagine that they use a language consisting of signs arbitrarily attached to things, unless we also attribute to them our power of discursive thought.

When, then, from this point of view we compare together instinct and intelligence, we see that each is a mode of psychical activity, and that while the one, instinct, is far more perfect than the other in its accomplishment of its purpose, far more complete in its insight, it is nevertheless confined to a very limited range; the other, far less perfect in accomplishing any purpose, far less complete in the insight it gives of reality, yet opens to our activity a practically unlimited range. They are also distinguished by their attitude. Instinct is sympathy. It is the feeling of the intimate bond that binds the individual to the reality. Intelligence is essentially external; it makes us regard reality as something other than our life, as something hostile that we may overcome.

CHAPTER IV

INTUITION

ALTHOUGH the two modes of mental activity, instinct and intelligence, in their perfect manifestation are so sharply distinguished from one another, yet they exist together in our consciousness in a very close and intimate union. For instinct is akin to that power of direct insight that we have called intuition. It is this power which in our view philosophy must make use of to seize again the simplicity of the reality that is in a manner distorted in the intelligent view of things. Intuition is that sympathetic attitude to the reality without us that makes us seem to enter into it, to be one with it, to live it. It is in contrast to the defiant attitude that we seem to assume when in science we treat facts and things as outside, external, discrete existences, which we range before us, analyse, discriminate, break up and re-combine. Intuition is not a new sense revealing to us unsuspected things or qualities of things. It is an aspect of conscious existence recognised in every philosophy. All that is new in Bergson's theory is the emphasis laid on intuition, and the suggestion that in it lies the possibility of the solution of the intellectual puzzle. What is new is not the recognition that there is an immediacy of feeling that precedes, forms

45

the basis of or is the substance of discursive thought, and accompanies it. What is new is the exhortation not to turn our backs on this immediacy in order to follow the method of science in the hope and expectation of finding a profounder and richer reality in the concepts of the understanding, the frames into which our intellect fits the reality, but to use the intuition to seize the reality itself, to make of intuition a philosophical instrument, to find in it a philosophical method. By so doing, and only by so doing, can we have a real metaphysic, a knowledge of things in themselves, a science that is beyond, or rather before, or perhaps we should say both before and beyond, the sciences. No one saw this need more clearly than did the philosopher Kant, to whom the problem of philosophy presented itself in a practically identical form to that in which Bergson presents it. Is a metaphysic possible ? Is it possible to know things in themselves, things as they are, without the space and time form in which our senses apprehend them, without the concepts in which our understanding frames them ? Kant thought it was not possible. There is no knowledge, he said, of things in themselves. The philosophy of Kant became, therefore, a theory of knowledge, but a theory of knowledge that involved the denial of knowledge. Theory of knowledge cannot stand alone. If all knowledge is relative, there is no knowledge. The immediate followers of Kant saw this, and sought the absolute—Fichte in the ego, Hegel in the logical idea itself, Schopenhauer in unconscious will. Bergson has perceived that there cannot be a theory of knowledge without a theory of life, that the two are inseparable, because it is for life that knowledge exists. Life is not known as an external thing, apprehended by the senses under a space form and a time form, fitted into the frames or shaped in the moulds that the intellect uses, but is directly known. The intuition of life is knowledge of reality itself, reality as it is in itself. But, on the other hand, we cannot have a theory of life that is not accompanied by a criticism of knowledge. It is theory of knowledge which enables us to see how the concepts of the understanding have been constructed, how they serve as a convenient and necessary symbolism for our positive science, how we may enlarge or go beyond them, and what is their true place in the evolution of life.

When I begin to learn a new language it appears to me as a vocabulary of words that I must commit to memory, with the rules for their use, the declensions and conjugations, the genders and cases, the construction of sentences, the idioms, the syntax, the spelling and the pronunciation. The task seems appalling. If I had to learn the language by committing to memory every word and every rule, I might by severe application get perhaps considerable knowledge of it, but it would be of a halting and practically useless kind. But what happens ? As soon as I begin to use the language, either by speaking or reading it, though I may only have acquired a few words and a slight knowledge of construction, I seem to enter into it, and it seems to form itself round me. It ceases to appear to me as arbitrary sounds and rules; it becomes a mode of expression. which continually, and as a whole, progresses to more and more perfect expression, and not by the mere addition to memory of words and rules. And on the other hand my own language which I learnt in early childhood without difficulty, because it formed itself round me and grew with my growth, this language, which forms so natural a part of my life that I cannot even in thought divest myself of it, for it is the vehicle of my thought, I can, when I will, set before myself and see it fall apart into sounds, combinations and rules. It is in the same way that intuition and intellect are blended in our life.

This applies to everything whatever that we know. There is a difference in the knowledge we have of anything that consists in the attitude towards it. When you are reading you hardly notice the sentences, words, letters, and the spaces dividing them, that compose the page and convey to you the author's meaning. You certainly do not notice that all you have before you is black marks on a white ground. Yet if you will you can present to yourself these, and these only, as the things you perceive. This very philosophy may appear to you as a set of very debateable propositions, none of which separately would bring conviction, and all of which in the aggregate would seem to lack cohesion, or you may enter sympathetically into it, find yourself at its point of view, find that it becomes the expression of your own attitude, and that it throws light for you on the whole problem of thought and existence. One thing is certain, that if you are convinced by this or any other philosophy, it is because you have entered into it by sympathy, and not because you have weighed its arguments as a set of abstract propositions.

But the clearest evidence of intuition is in the works of great artists. What is it that we call genius in great painters and poets and musicians ? It is the power they have of seeing more than we see, and of enabling us by their expression to penetrate further into reality. What they see is there to be seen, but only they see it because they are gifted with a higher power than we. What is the more that is revealed to them ? It is not scientific truth, nor is it technical skill, for this is a consequence, not a cause of genius. It is the power to enter by sympathy into their subject. Great art is inspiration, it is the power to know whatever subject engages it by entering within it and living its life. What makes the artist's picture ? Not the colours which he mixes on his palette and transfers to his canvas—these are only his means of expression—not the model which sits to give him direction in his composition, nor the skill with which he portrays the reality in his representation; what makes the picture is the artist's vision, his entry into the very life of his subject by sympathy, something that he never succeeds in expressing perfectly, though the imperfect expression may reveal to us more than we could see without it.

A symphony does not consist in the vibration of strings and reeds and stretched skins and tubes which give it expression, nor does its interpretation

D

consist in the skill with which the performers mani-
pulate the instruments that produce the vibrations.
The work is an individual, indivisible whole which
the composer has created and the performers apprehend, and not the aggregate of discrete sounds into
which it can at any time be decomposed. It is
known directly in one intuition. Intuition is the
entering into it as distinct from the standing over
against it and watching its successive parts or select-
ing points of view of it.

What purpose, then, does the intellect serve ?
Why do we distort, or at least transform, reality ?
Or—if this seems, as indeed it is, an extreme way of
stating it—why does the intellect involve us in the
illusion that the continuous is discrete, that the
moving and changing is at rest ? What is the
advantage that intellectual frames give us ? Bergson
in his answer to these questions has shown us both
why and how these things can be. His answer is
entirely original. The problems are old enough, but
the solution now offered in this philosophy has not
been propounded before. It is the theory of life
that offers the solution of the problem of knowledge.
Clearly if the whole end and purpose of our being
were knowledge, if knowledge were an end and not
merely the means to an end, these frames would
not only be useless, but a positive hindrance. If the
end of knowledge were the contemplation of eternal
truth, it is intuition alone that would serve that
end, the intellect would be a stumbling-block. But
our theory of life shows us knowing as a means not
an end, it is for the sake of acting. How, then,

does knowledge serve action, and in what special way does intellectual knowledge serve action better than intuitional knowledge ? The illustrations we have already given may indicate the answer. The intellect gives us the same advantage over intuition that the material tool gives to us as compared with the organical tool that the insect possesses. It opens a practically unlimited range to our activity. It supplies us with a symbolism, a language, a system of detached and detachable signs which enables us to use our experience to guide our present action. It gives us the sciences. The sciences are the organisation of experience into systems of reality that serve the mind as tools serve the body. We are continually confronted with the need of action ; while we live there is this unceasing demand to act. There seem to be only two ways in which we may be qualified to meet this demand ; one is by a direct intuition which drives us to act in one path and one only, the other is by the intellect which ranges before us our experience and enables us to choose from many possible courses the one that offers best hope of success. How could this be unless our actions, accomplished and contemplated, could be presented before us as individual unities, and the sphere of our activity as ends and motives ? This the intellect does. It articulates the living flow, makes the past appear as successive events, the present as simultaneous positions or situations of definite things, and so enables us to search in the past for identical situations to guide us, to recognise similarities in the present, and to anticipate in the future the results of our activity as actions accomplished. And the articulations that the intellect makes in the living flow are natural articulations because they follow the practical needs of our nature, but they are not absolute, for with other needs there would be other divisions. There is no absolutely formless reality; the presence of one form is the absence of another, but the lines and divisions are the necessities that human activity demands.

Without intellect our life would lack all that order which appears to us in the form of successive events, all the divisions and lines that seem to us the actual articulations of the inert material world, but life would exist. Life, the concrete reality, itself is not a formless chaos, not a manifold without order nor a unity without form, but an absolute that holds in itself the possibility of all form. We cannot represent it or imagine it without form, and for the power to represent and imagine at all we are dependent on the intellect, but we can distinguish the form that the intellect gives it, and see in the purpose that the intellect serves the reason of that form. And also we can know life without intellectual form, for consciousness of living is the intuition of life.

But if reality is life, and if the solid things and their relations are the order that the intellect discerns in this reality, what is the nothing that stands opposed to this reality, what is the disorder that is the alternative to this order ? It seems to us that when we think that something exists we can equally think that it does not exist, and when we think of any arrangement or order we can equally think of

the absence of order. The opposite of reality is
nothing, the opposite of order is disorder, and so we
seem to have positive ideas of nothing and of disorder. And so we ask questions that seem to touch
the very depth of the problem of existence. Why is
there any reality at all ? Why does something exist
rather than nothing ? Why is there order in reality
rather than disorder ? When we characterise reality
as life, the question seems so much more pressing,
for the subject of it seems so much fuller of content
than when we set over against one another bare
abstract categories, like the being and the nothing
that Hegel declared to be identical. It seems easy
to imagine that life might cease and then nothing
would remain. In this way we come to picture to
ourselves a nought spread out beneath reality, a
reality that has come to be and that might cease to
be, and then again there would be nought. This idea
of an absolute nothing is a false idea, arising from
an illusion of the understanding. Absolute nothing
is unthinkable. The problems that arise out of the
idea we seem to have of it are unmeaning. It is
very important to understand this point if we would
grasp the full meaning of the theory of knowledge.
Behind the reality which we know there is no non-
being that we can think of as actually taking its
place, and also there is no actual chaos or confusion
or disorder which we can think of as taking the
place of the order which we know, and which would
be the condition of reality without that order.
Bergson is not the first who has discovered that we
cannot have an idea of nothing, but no one has

exposed so forcibly and so clearly the misapprehension that rests on this false idea. It is very easy to see that it must be a false idea. Every idea is an idea of something, every feeling is a feeling of something, nothing is not something, and therefore to think of absolute nothing is not to think, to feel nothing is not to feel. But we think we are thinking of something when we think of an actual nothing; what is it that we think of ? It is the absence of something. We can think that any particular thing that exists might not exist; what we are then thinking of is the general reality with this particular thing absent. We can extend this thought to include the non-existence of all that is, but what then ? We find that we are thinking of all reality as absent and ourself looking on at the void which we imagine. It is not a positive nothing that is in our thought; the present reality is in our thought, and without its presence we could not picture a void. Absolute nought is unimaginable and inconceivable. Now try and realise the importance of this for our theory. Reality is not a thing in itself which exists, we know not why, and which might equally well not exist. The living reality which intuition reveals to us is absolute, its non-existence cannot be imagined or conceived. So also with the order that we perceive in it; it is the direction of our interest as individuals of the human species, the articulation which serves our activity; but the absence of this order would be the presence of some other order, there is no positive disorder on which order is imposed. When we see clearly that the idea of the nought and

the idea of disorder are false ideas, we can dismiss
as entirely without meaning problems that have
filled a large place in philosophy and that are per-
sistent in ordinary thought. Was creation out of
nothing, or has something existed from eternity ?
Was there an original formless matter on which
order has been imposed ? Such questions arise in
false ideas, and have no answer because they have
no meaning.

The perception that reality is that which we cannot
even in thought imagine non-existent, that the only
alternative to the order that we recognise in this
reality is not a positive disorder but some other
order, alters profoundly the whole problem of philosophy as it has hitherto been presented. We have
no longer to explain a dualism. The intuition of
reality that we have in the consciousness of our own
life is not the apprehension of a kind of reality
altogether different from that other reality which we
know when we perceive external things. Space is
not one reality and time another. It is one identical
reality that we know by intuition in life, by understanding in physical science. The point of view at
which matter and mind appear to be two realities
different in their nature, impossible to reduce to an
identity, and yet in some mysterious way in close
relation, this view which has been the starting-point
of philosophy since Descartes, and which has in one
form or another given its problem to philosophy
ever since, is simply superseded. The philosophy of
Bergson is not a reconciliation of this old problem
of dualism; what it does is to offer us a point of

view from which the problem does not and cannot arise. Hence its peculiar significance and immense importance. It is in very truth a new departure. It is not a new light on old problems; it is a new principle of interpretation, suggested and made possible by the enormous advance of the biological sciences in modern times.

CHAPTER V

FREEDOM

THE question of most vital interest to each of us as individual living beings, that concerns us most intimately in its practical as well as its speculative interest, is the question of freewill. Are we free agents, or only creatures of circumstance ? Is the choice that seems at every moment open to us real or only apparent ? Could an omniscient mind, knowing the present conditions of the universe, foretell the next and every future state ? Or, is there in free action something entirely undetermined, and therefore unpredictable ? Am I actually free, or is my liberty of action only ignorance of conditions that determine my actions even to the minutest details ? The tremendous moral consequences that seem to be involved in this problem of freewill have made it one of the most debated controversies in philosophy. And it is one of those problems that seem beyond the power of human reason to bring to a satisfactory solution. The terms are simple enough, and there is no question, so far as the main controversy is concerned, of any ambiguity in what is meant. Yet we may prove, as Jonathan Edwards, the eighteenth-century American theologian, did, by the most simple and unanswerable logic, and by an argument that appeals with full force to both parties, that freewill is impossible—it is no use, it is like proving that Achilles cannot overtake the tortoise; there rises up against the argument a feeling that claims all the authority of fact, and seems to turn the reasoning to foolishness. Is it possible to explain the persistence of this everlasting problem? May it be that there is a confusion in the meaning of the terms, a contradiction in the very heart of the problem? May it be that there is an illusion in our common way of thinking of things, and that this illusion once removed, this and other problems will lose their meaning and disappear?

The problem of freewill or determinism is generally stated in such a way that the case for freewill is made impossible by the very form of the question. We ask, can we choose indifferently between two alternatives, or must the strongest motive prevail? But such a question is unreal, for there is no other test of the strongest motive but the fact that we choose it. The freewill supposed in a choice that is indifferent to motives is also absurd in its ethical aspect, for the moral responsibility of the agent which it is supposed to establish is clearly destroyed. What we really mean when we ask, Are we free? is, whether when we act we really create, or whether creation is impossible; not whether any action is undetermined, but whether every action can be predicted beforehand as certainly as its conditions are determined once it is carried out. The view of this philosophy is that life is creation, and that the reality of the universe is incessant creation. This idea is Bergson's central conception towards which all his arguments converge.]

The illusion that gives rise to the problem of free-will is the mental picture that we form of time. The time that we ordinarily think about is not real time, but a picture of space. In ordinary thought and language we represent space and time as each a homogeneous medium, that is to say, as two realities in which all the parts are of exactly the same kind as one another, in which there are no actual differences nor divisions between one part and another part. Differences and divisions all belong to the objects and events that fill them, not to space and time themselves. In space, material objects lie outside one another, and in time, conscious states succeed one another. Now the time which we imagine as a medium in which events happen, or, as we say (using a spatial image), take place, is only a symbolical representation of space. When we think of states succeeding one another, we are not thinking of time at all, but of space. Real time, the true duration, is entirely different; it is not a succession, but, like life or consciousness, an existence in which all reality is the actually present, moving, changing, now. In consciousness states do not lie outside one another but interpenetrate, and the whole undivided consciousness changes without ceasing. Now whenever we think of change as the succession of fixed states we think of these states as lying beside one another, and change as the passing from one to the other. This is not real change. It is only in space that one thing is outside another thing, and when we repre-

sent states as separate things, whether we imagine
them to exist side by side or to follow one another,
we are using a spatial symbol, and the succession
of states is only a picture of ourself passing from
one thing to another thing in space. In real change
there are no states at all; everything is a living,
moving present. Existence in time is life. It is
very important to grasp this point clearly; it is so
fundamental, that unless it is understood and accepted,
it is little likely that the subsequent arguments will
carry conviction. And it is not an easy doctrine to
explain or to understand, for the very language in
which alone we can express it is steeped in spatial
symbolism. Language seems to require us to make
the same sharp distinction between our ideas that
we make between material objects. It is when we
grasp the true nature of our experience of time, and
distinguish it from the spatial representation of it,
that is indeed both useful in practice and necessary
in science, that the real nature of freewill appears.
It is this spatial time that makes us think of ourselves as made up of elements that can be measured
and counted like material objects, and of our actions
as the play of these elements. When we see that
life and consciousness are not measurable at all,
that it is always something else that we are measuring
when we think that we are comparing or counting
conscious states, that they are not quantities but
pure qualities, not outside of and distinct from one
another, but interpenetrating and permeating the
living individual who progresses and develops, the
old problem of determinism disappears, and freewill

is seen to be the creative power of the individual who is one and indivisible.

Freewill, as this philosophy affirms it, is creative action. All the actions that we perform, all the actions that, taken together, make up our individual lives, are not free actions. Our free actions are very rare, and for the vast mass of mankind may even not exist at all. And, moreover, it is not possible to pick out of our lives certain actions and say of them, these are, what the rest are not, free. When we regard our individual actions and analyse them into means and ends and purposes, the determinist argument is inevitable. Whether we regard only the physical causation that is involved in every action, or whether we think of the psychical causation involved in the motives and ends and purposes that constitute the alternatives from which we choose, there is no way of resisting the determinist conclusion that all our actions can only be explained by their conditions, and these conditions leave no place for freewill, as determinists and indeterminists alike have defined it. But what is true of the parts viewed as parts is not necessarily true of the whole. And so it may be that when we regard our action as a chain of complementary parts linked together, each action so viewed is rigidly conditioned, yet when we regard our whole life as one and indivisible, it may be free. So also with the life which we hold to be the reality of the universe; when we view it in its detail as the intellect presents it to us, it appears as an order of real conditioning, each separate state having its ground in an antecedent state, yet as a whole, as the living impulse, it is free and creative. We are free when our acts spring from our whole personality, when they express that personality. These acts are not unconditioned, but the conditions are not external, but in our character, which is ourself.

Freewill, this power of free creative action, is not the liberty of choice that indeterminists have asserted and determinists have denied. It is not the feeling of liberty that we have when we are set face to face with alternative courses from which to choose, nor is it the feeling we have when our choice has been made and we look back on the action accomplished, the feeling that we need not have acted as we did and could have acted differently. Freewill is the very nature of our lives as individual wholes, the expression of the individuality of life. Our actions, even our free creative actions, follow from and depend upon our character, and our character is formed by circumstances, but it is not external to us, it is ourself. But it is only at times that free action is called for. Our ordinary life is made up of actions that are largely automatic, of habits and conventions that form a crust around our free expression; it is only at moments of crisis or when we are touched with deep emotion that we seem to burst through this crust and our whole self decides our action. But further, as this philosophy shows, there is that in the nature of life and consciousness which is itself essentially freewill. Causality is a scientific conception, and science is an intellectual view. Physical science is the order that the intellect imposes on the flowing. The intellect finds resemblances, binds like to like, organises experience into systems in which recognised antecedents have recognised consequents, and so makes prediction possible. And it extends this view to the living world and to the conscious world of thought and will. But life itself, as we know it in intuition, is not like this intellectual view of it; it is a becoming in which there is no repetition, in which, therefore, prediction is impossible, for it is continual new creation.

Freewill is only possible, therefore, if the intellectual view is not absolute. There is no place for it in the world as physical science presents it. And consequently to prove that the will is free is to prove that we have a spiritual as distinct from a material nature, that we are not merely mechanical arrangements of parts in a block universe, but living upholders of a universe that is open to our creative activity.

But even so, is this liberty so very important? Do we not share it with everything that lives? If we have acquired an advantage which has made us lords of the surface of this planet, it is but a little difference that parts us from the lower and less successful forms. If the reality is the life that has evolved us, and this life imparts to us a portion of its own essential freedom, is it not imparted for a purely practical reason, and does not everything that lives share it in some degree? Are not the limitations so overwhelming that the consciousness of this rare freedom hardly counts against the obstacles that block its exercise? Is not the superiority that seems to raise us above all other living beings merely our point of view due to the narrowness of our outlook ? It may be so, but there is also reason to think that our human life is something more than the success of a species by natural selection in the struggle for existence Humanity may be in a special sense the triumph of the life impulse itself. I will give this idea in Bergson's own words : " From our point of view, life appears in its entirety as an immense wave which, starting from a centre, spreads outwards, and which on almost the whole of its circumference is stopped and converted into oscillation ; at one single point the obstacle has been forced, the impulsion has passed freely. It is this freedom that the human form registers. Everywhere but in man consciousness has had to come to a stand ; in man alone it has kept on its way. Man, then, continues the vital movement indefinitely, although he does not draw along with him all that life carries in itself. On other lines of evolution there have travelled other tendencies which life implied, and of which, since everything interpenetrates, man has, doubtless, kept something, but of which he has kept only very little. It is as if a vague and formless being, whom we may call, as we will, man or superman, had sought to realise himself, and had succeeded only by abandoning a part of himself on the way." (*Creative Evolution*, p. 280.)

CHAPTER VI

MIND AND BODY

THERE are two guiding principles in Bergson's philosophy: the one is that knowledge is for the sake of action, and the other is that this practical purpose of knowledge leads to habits of thought which create fictitious problems. We have seen that the problem of the freedom of the will as it has been presented hitherto in philosophy alike by determinists and indeterminists is one of these fictitious problems. Another is the problem underlying the controversy between Idealism and Realism that has had so large a place in philosophy, ancient and modern. Impressions from the outer world seem to come to us by our senses and to be transmitted along our nerves to our brain, and to be there in some way transformed into perceptions of things. And the problem of psychology has been to understand how this can be. The idealist, insisting on the fact that the only actual reality is the perception in the mind, holds that the mind must in some way project these perceptions outside itself, and so build up what we call the external world. The realist, on the other hand, insists that the object is an independent thing of which the mind has a perception, but he cannot explain how a perception formed in the mind, or it may be in the brain, can agree with a real object that is entirely independent of the mind and the brain. He is led to propound theories of which that known as the " epiphenomenon " may be quoted as an example, in which it is supposed that the vibrations transmitted through the molecules of the brain-cells produce a kind of phosphorescence or luminous trail, which is the perception of things. Now idealism and realism alike rest on the view that the brain is in some sort of way a manufactory in which perceptions are produced, notwithstanding that the idealist is bound to regard the brain and the movements in the brain as themselves perceptions, and the realist is bound to regard the brain as only one among other objects, and can give no reason why it should, or how it can, have the power or function of reproducing or representing all other objects. Both idealists and realists regard memories as a kind of perception, and consider one of the functions of the brain is to store the perceptions it has given rise to, and reproduce them as recollections on occasion. In Bergson's view this whole conception of the function of the brain is false. The brain is not a manufactory of ideas nor a storehouse of memories. It is a kind of telephonic exchange. The body is organised for action, the impressions which pass into the body are already perceptions, they are incentives to action, and the function of the brain is to respond to them by setting going the appropriate action.

I will now try and explain as simply and concisely

as I can what, for this philosophy, perception is and
what memory is, what the body is and what the
mind is, what is matter and what is spirit, and what
is the function that the body performs.

When we are conscious we perceive and we recollect. We never perceive anything without at the
same time remembering, but though perception and
memory always exist together in conscious experience, they are different in kind from one another,
and must be dissociated to be understood. A
memory is not a weaker kind of perception, and a
perception is not an intenser memory. A pure perception is the immediate and instantaneous vision of
matter that I might imagine myself to have if I
were living entirely in the present without any
memory. If I disregard all philosophical theories,
and try to represent the universe as it appears to me,
it will seem to consist of a great variety of objects,
one of which is my body. My body differs from the
other objects in this, that while the other objects
act and react on one another according to constant
laws which I call laws of nature, my body seems to
have the power of performing new and original
actions. My body is a centre of action. It receives
movements from the objects round me and gives
back movement to them. This is performed by
means of the nervous system, at the centre of which
is a highly complex structure, the brain. All movements do not pass through the brain; some go to the
spinal cord, and are immediately and automatically
converted into actions; those that pass through the
brain are perceived before they are converted into

actions. And so it seems to me that the brain must produce perceptions. But the function of the brain is simply to transmit movement, and its great complexity is to give me choice of movement. In order to choose, consciousness must perceive, but perceptions would not serve action if they were manufactured in the brain. To be of use to me perceptions must come to me from the objects round me and among which my action is to take place. I perceive in the world around me not the whole of reality, but that part of it which interests me on account of my possible action, the action that my body, having received the stimulus, will eventually perform. Perceptions are the movements from the objects outside my body, and my brain acts as a dark screen, which throws up the image and illuminates it for consciousness. The function of my body is to select. Those movements that do not interest me with regard to possible action are reflected back, those that concern me pass in and are consciously perceived. This is why perceptions vary with the movements of my body, although they are not in the body, but outside me in the objects that I perceive. If the nerves that transmit the movements to the brain are divided my perceptions are destroyed, for the movements cannot reach the brain, and the brain cannot therefore set my body in motion. Perception is my actual present contact with the world in which my actions are taking place. In conscious experience there is no perception without memory. However instantaneous perception may seem it has some duration, and all duration is the existence of the past in the present. Pure perception, which exists in theory only, is what the present would be if it retained nothing of the past. Its reality is its activity. The past is idea, the present is movement. In perception we touch and penetrate and live the reality of things. When we perceive we do not, as the idealist supposes, construct or reconstruct things, nor do we, as the realist supposes, only represent them.

As pure perception is wholly in the present, so pure memory is wholly in the past. The past is that which has ceased to act, it has not ceased to exist. The whole of our past perceptions survive their active living present and exist, in the order and with the circumstances of their occurrence, in the form of unconscious psychical states. The mind plays in regard to this time existence an exactly similar part to that which the body plays in regard to the perception of present images in space. It enables us to forget. It shuts out from consciousness all past recollections which do not interest the present action, and it brings into consciousness those recollections which serve the purpose of present activity. These blend with and interpret and become one with the present action, and therefore it is that in actual experience neither present perception nor memory is ever pure. There is no past perception which may not be, under some necessity, brought by the mind into present consciousness, but because we are not conscious of a recollection until it is present, we think that it is only when we are conscious of it that it exists. We think therefore that it is a new and different existence, and not something that already existed in the unconscious.

This theory of pure memory is an essential doctrine in Bergson's philosophy, and it is the most revolutionary compared with hitherto accepted psychological theory. The very affirmation of the existence of unconscious psychical states seems to involve a contradiction in terms, for consciousness is generally held to be an essential property of psychical states. But, according to Bergson, this is due to our regarding consciousness as a function that is only accidentally practical, and that is really intended to give us pure knowledge, and therefore we think that there can be nothing real in consciousness that is not actual. But the unconscious plays in perception an exactly similar part to that which it plays in memory. When I perceive any object, I am unconscious of all but a very small part of the existence which I perceive. All these things that I am unconscious of form part of the present existence that I perceive. So also when I recollect any past event, I am unconscious of all but a very small part of the existence which seems to be spread out behind me in the past.

It is this refusal to recognise the existence of unconscious psychical states, to recognise the reality of what Bergson names spirit, that compels us to suppose that memories are preserved in the matter of the brain, either by being stored up in cells, or by being the molecular paths that perception has traced. A large part of *Matter and Memory* is devoted to an examination and criticism of the various forms of this theory, and also to an account of recent actual experimental research which seems to prove that the theory in any form must be wrong even on strictly scientific grounds.

Pure memory, therefore, affirms the existence of mind or spirit, an existence that cannot be reduced to or explained by matter. But there are two forms of memory; only one of them is pure memory. When I have learnt a poem or a musical composition by heart I say that I remember it, but memory in this case refers to the present and the future and not to the past; that which I remember has become a whole for me that I retain and can repeat when I will. It is true that I have had to learn it, and those efforts are past, but the memory is a present possession. Each of those efforts, however, is a personal memory, a picture image with its particular outline, colour, and place in time, individual and unique, and not to be repeated. These two forms of memory always exist together in our experience, but they are radically different from one another; the one is a formed motor habit, a mechanism, a habit interpreted by memory; the other is true memory, an existence in time.

Perception affirms the reality of matter, memory affirms the reality of spirit. Are we not then confronted with the problems and difficulties that have always seemed inseparable from dualism ? No, because both perception and memory serve a practical purpose; they prepare us for and direct our actions, they unite in the reality of the movement that is life. We have not, on the one hand, a series of mechanical movements, and, on the other, a series of psychical states with no common measure between them. We have not, as in idealist and realist theories, two realities, the only function of one of which is to know the other. Quite different is the view that Bergson gives of the function of the body in the life of the spirit.

Our body is the exact actual present point at which our action is taking place, the point at which perception marks out our possible actions, and memory brings the weight, as it were, of the past to push us forward as we advance into the future. The body is our instrument of action, it is the sharp edge of the knife which cuts into the future. At every moment it may be said to perish and to be born again. It is the moving point pressing forward, the present moment in which consciousness makes that instantaneous section across the universal becoming which takes for us the form of solid matter spread out in space. This is why we experience it in two ways, by external sensations which present it as an object among other objects, and by internal feelings, pleasure and pain, which make it for us a privileged object known from within.

What, then, is the reality that we perceive ? The reality is movement. Movements are indivisible and occupy duration. Our life is an indivisible movement, and the universal becoming is composed of movements. To perceive is to form these movements into objects and things, just as in the consciousness of a flash of light billions of successive vibrations are condensed into one sensation. Our body is at the actual point where the present advancing into the future is becoming the past, and at this point perception makes a cut across the universal flow. This present reality is matter. Matter is the section which we imagine to exist simultaneously at every moment of actual perception, and as this centre of perception moves forward the whole section seems to move with it. Space is the way in which we represent it. Space is the continuity which seems to underlie matter. It is the symbol which makes it possible to the mind to represent to itself this section. And so space seems not to perish and be born again with each new moment, but to be an independent, indestructible reality underlying the universe. And the past and the future we represent by a similar symbol that we call time. We represent time as a continuity which underlies the succession of our states, and it seems to be an independent reality that spreads like space, only that it is behind us and before us instead of around us.

The things into which external perception divides matter are the lines that mark out our possible actions. There is no absolute form in the sense of a fixity of things. The reality flows. Our individual lives are indivisible movements each with its own quality, and around us are movements also indivisible and qualitative, and all form one reality of becoming that endures and grows in the manner of a consciousness. The outlines of things that external perception presents to us are not absolute, but relative to our bodily needs and functions. The fundamental conditions of perception concern the

uses to be made of things, the practical advantage
to be drawn from them.

What, then, is spirit? It is the progress, the
evolution, the prolonging of the past into the present.
It is a pure time existence. It unites with matter
in the act of perception, but the union can only be
expressed in terms of time and not in terms of space.
It is the memory which holds the past and unites it
with the present in the living reality.

CHAPTER VII

CREATIVE EVOLUTION

In the latter half of last century, and following the formulation of the great scientific generalisation of the evolution of living species, the philosophy of Herbert Spencer seemed to promise to found on the principle of evolution a new synthesis of knowledge. Whatever our view of the permanent value of Herbert Spencer's work, it cannot be denied that the wonderful promise that it seemed to contain was not fulfilled, and the hope and enthusiasm that it inspired was followed by disappointment. And now again evolution is the principle of a new construction, and the basis of a philosophy. But this philosophy is not a mere classification and generalisation of the results of the sciences, it explains the sciences by showing the genesis of matter in the reality of life. What is the difference between the two methods? It may be summed up in the word "creative." In this is revealed the true nature of evolution. Spencer recognised the fact that the world and the living forms it contained were the result of evolution, and he thought it was sufficient to break up and dissociate into simpler elements the world that had been evolved in order to show its evolution. His method was to cut up the present evolved reality into little bits, though the little bits must themselves have been evolved, and then re-compose the reality with the fragments. In so doing he did not see that he was positing in advance everything that there was to be explained. The true evolution must explain the genesis of nat-- and of mind. Herbert Spencer's principle of evolution never freed itself from the vice of mechanical explanation. The future and the past could all be calculated from the present. All is given. Time does nothing, and therefore is nothing. This is essentially the scientific method of explanation. And the attempt to interpret it by adding the idea of purpose or final cause does not alter its character. It introduces a psychological element, but it remains essentially a mechanical explanation, except that the conditions of present existence are placed partly in the future instead of wholly in the past.

True evolution is creative. We have seen that life and consciousness have no meaning unless time is real. The same is true of evolution. If time is a succession of real things and not itself a reality, if the continued creation of the world means that it dies and is re-born at every instant, there is no evolution. Evolution implies a real persistence of the past in the present, a duration which is not an interval between two states, but which links them together. The principle then of this philosophy is that reality is time, that it can only be expressed in terms of time, that there is no stuff more resistant nor more substantial than time, that it is the very stuff of which life and consciousness are made.

Evolution is creative; in organic evolution as in consciousness the past presses against the present and causes the upspringing of a new form incommensurable with its antecedents. In the primitive impulse must be sought the solution of the problem of organic evolution.

The problem is to account for the variations of living beings together with the persistence of their type, the origin, in a word, of species. There are three present forms of evolutionist theory—the neo-Darwinian, according to which the essential causes of variation are the differences inherent in the germ borne by the individual, and not the experience or behaviour of the individual in the course of his career ; the theory known as Orthogenesis, according to which there is a continual changing in a definite direction from generation to generation ; and the neo-Lamarckian theory, according to which the cause of variation is the conscious effort of the individual, an effort passed on to descendants. Each of these theories may be true to the extent that it explains certain facts, but there are two difficulties that no one of the theories nor all together can surmount. One of these is the fact that the development of exactly similar organs is found on quite distinct and widely separated lines of evolution. There is a striking example of this in the Pecten, the common mollusc that we call the scollop, which has eyes the structure of which is identical with the vertebrate eye in its minutest details, yet the eye of the mollusc and the eye of the vertebrate must have been developed quite independently of one another, and ages after each had left the parent stock. The other difficulty is that in all organic evolution an infinite complexity of structure is combined with an absolute simplicity of function. Thus the variation of an organ like the eye cannot be a single variation, but must involve the simultaneous occurrence of an infinite number of variations all coordinated to the single purpose of vision, which is a simple function. These are facts that can only be explained by the hypothesis of an original impetus retaining its direction in channels far removed and divided from their common source.

Life is an original impetus. It is not the mere heading of a class of things that live. We may picture it as a visible current, taking its rise at a certain moment, in a certain point of space, passing from generation to generation, dividing and diverging, losing nothing of its force, but intensifying in proportion to its advance. If now we continue this simile, and try to picture the course of evolution on the surface of this planet, it seems to us that it must have commenced with a very humble effort, life stooping, as it were, to insinuate itself into the interstices of resisting matter, for the earliest forms of life appear to have been very lowly. Yet from the first life had within it that tremendous push which was destined to carry it to the highest forms. Its progress seems to have been always by dissociation, by dividing, by diverging, by parting with some of its powers in order to emphasise others, but always retaining something of the whole in every part. So we see the first great subdivision into the vegetable and the animal, each distinguished not so much by positive characteristics as by divergent tendencies, the one a tendency towards immobility and unconscious torpor, the other towards mobility and consciousness, and both at the same time complementary as well as opposed to one another. In the development of animal life we see this same continual divergence. On many lines the progress has been arrested or even turned back, but along two main lines it has found free way, the line of the vertebrates at the end of which we ourselves stand, and the line of the arthropods that has found its highest expression in the ants and the bees. In these two lines of evolution we find the perfecting of two modes of activity, instinct and intelligence. In the vital impulsion that from the first early simple form of a living cell has developed the multitude of forms that have been and now are existing on our planet we may distinguish three elements, elements that coincided in the common impetus but have been dissociated by the very fact of their growth. These are the unconscious sleep of the vegetable and the instinct and intelligence of the animal. They are not, as the common opinion has been, three successive degrees of the development of one tendency, but three divergent directions of an activity that has split up as it grew.

From this standpoint of the ordinary observation of life we see that these modes of the vital activity are not things that life has produced for their own sake, not the final realisations of a purpose. They are not things nor ends, but tendencies. They are an intimate part of the vital activity, the means by which it pushes on its ceaseless movement. Intelligence and instinct are not separated by sharply drawn distinctions. They are different tendencies, entirely different in the mode of their activity, but they exist together, commingled and interpenetrating. Neither one nor the other exists for the sake of pure speculative knowledge. Each gives a knowledge that is subservient to life, and that knowledge is directed to giving the living creature command over the matter that seems to resist and oppose his progress. Such in brief is the conclusion which we reach when we study the evolution of life as it appears to ordinary observation and to science. It suggests a certain conception of knowledge, and this again implies a metaphysics, and thus we are brought to philosophy.

Ordinary observation therefore without any philosophical presuppositions shows us that there is a current of life that from lowly beginnings has pushed on its course, creating ever new forms in its passage from generation to generation, and this current seems to have had to meet and overcome a resisting current, which to our view seems immense in comparison and overwhelming, a universe of solid matter spread out in a boundless space. And in this current of life we may distinguish in particular two modes of conscious activity, instinct and intelligence, which stand out as different directions of activity from a background of consciousness in general. What we call in distinction to matter, mind, is larger than intellect, larger also than instinct.

We now come to the special task of philosophy, which is to show the genesis of intellectuality and of materiality in the one reality of life ; to show that the two currents, the advancing current and the resisting or opposing current, are one movement, the difference being in their direction alone ; to show how this movement is brought about by the interruption of the one movement. To accomplish this task the work of philosophy is twofold; it must combine with a criticism of knowledge a metaphysic, that is to say, a mental grasp or conception of the reality which transcends the intellect.

Never surely was so tremendous an undertaking entered upon with such direct simplicity as Bergson has done in the third chapter of *Creative Evolution*. The attempt to engender the intellect itself may appear more daring than the boldest speculations of metaphysicians, but it is in reality much more modest. So he describes the work, and truly he is right. It is because philosophers have taken intelligence as already given, and by it or from it have sought to explain, or even to construct, the whole of reality, that their efforts have been unavailing. It is by abasing the claims of reason, by stooping, that we conquer.

It is instinct and intelligence that give the clue. They stand out from a background that we may call consciousness in general, and which in the view of this philosophy is co-extensive with universal life. To show the genesis of consciousness we must set out from this general consciousness which embraces it. The intellect marks out to us the general form

F

of our action on matter, and the detail of matter is ruled by the requirements of our action. Hence there is a reciprocal adaptation, both intellect and matter are derived from a higher and wider existence.

But here an initial difficulty has probably already occurred to the reader. How is it possible for the intellect to discover the genesis of the intellect ? Does it not involve us in a vicious circle ? Even if there be a wider consciousness, I cannot divest myself of my intellectual apprehension in order to view my intellect from some other standpoint. The vicious circle is only in appearance however ; it is not real, because the intellect is not different from the wider consciousness. It is a nucleus, a condensation, a focussing, and the wider consciousness which surrounds it is of the same nature as itself. But on the other hand the vicious circle is real for every method in philosophy that regards the intellect as absolute and as given. For all such there is, as Kant most clearly proved, no metaphysic possible, that is to say, no grasp of a reality that is wider than the intellect. This is of such fundamental importance for the appreciation of Bergson's method that I must try to illustrate it. In the evolutionist philosophy of Herbert Spencer we are shown matter obeying laws, objects and facts connected by constant relations, and consciousness receiving the imprint of these laws and relations, and so shaping itself into intellect. But clearly the intellect which is supposed to arise in this way is already presupposed in the matter we speak of as objects and acts. What are objects and facts but our concepts

of matter ? Instead of showing how intelligence
arises, we assume it in the very conception of the
nature from which we seek to derive it. The same
holds true of those philosophies that start with consciousness and construct nature out of the categories
of thought. All suppose that the faculty of knowing
is co-extensive with the whole of experience, and they
must therefore explain away matter or explain away
mind or accept a dualism of two substances. This
philosophy, on the contrary, can accept the reality
of both matter and mind, and it shows how intellect
and matter arise by mutual adaptation, each pre-
supposing the other.

The evolution of life suggests to us, then, a certain
conception of knowledge and also a certain metaphysic, which imply each other. The conception of
knowledge is that the intellect is a special function
of the mind, that its essence is to comprehend
matter, that matter does not determine the form of
the intellect, nor does the intellect impose its form
on matter, nor is there any kind of pre-established
harmony between them, but that intellect and matter
have adapted themselves to one another. And the
metaphysical theory is that the intellectuality of the
mind and the materiality of things are not due to
separate substances, mind and matter, nor are they
even distinct movements, but two processes in one
movement. Each is an opposite direction of the
identical movement that is the other.

Let us first try and see what exactly matter is in
direct experience. When we concentrate our attention on our innermost experience, we perceive the

reality of our life as a pure duration in which the past as memory exists in the present and presses forward with the whole activity of our will into the future. There is one point, one sharp point, in our existence which marks the actually present moment. If we try to concentrate our being on that point, to think away all memory and all will, we can never quite succeed, but in the effort we may catch a glimpse of that pure present reality into which all actuality is gathered. It will appear, when no memory links it to the past, no will impels it to the future, as a momentary existence which dies and is re-born endlessly. It is at that point that matter exists as fixed, external, timeless states. If we could see that momentary existence, it is pure materiality that we should see. Life materialises at the point at which it is acting. At that point the changing flow assumes the form of solid external states, and the essential function of the intellect, the function for which it is peculiarly adapted, is to apprehend the reality in that form.

Our intellect then is the faculty of knowing matter in the form of extension in space. Science is the work of the intellect. In geometry its success is most complete, for geometry deals with pure space. The operations of the intellect tend to geometry, they are a kind of natural geometry. We see this even in logic, which is the pure science of thought itself. An ordered world of fixed states and constant laws is essential to the special form of our activity. The intellect shows us this order by apprehending reality in concepts which are the frames or moulds in which it fixes the flowing. It classifies and divides, cuts out systems in which causes are followed by effects, and in which the same effects are the result of the same causes. With unorganised matter it is completely successful, and we only perceive its limitations when we deal with the sciences of life. The positive sciences when they treat unorganised matter are in touch with actual reality. The order that the intellect shows us in nature is a real order, not a subjectively imposed order that exists only in our mind. It is an order that it finds, not merely an order that it gives, by saying which we affirm that the adaptation is mutual. The reality is both a material order and an intellectual order. The difficulty we find in accepting this important conclusion is due to an illusion of thought. We persist in thinking that order is something imposed on reality, and that without an imposed order there would be a disorder. The idea of disorder is purely relative to our interest; it is the absence of the order that we are seeking. The absence of an order we expect to find is the presence of a different order.

I will now try to make clear in a few words the most difficult, but at the same time the most important, idea in this philosophy, the idea that takes us to the very depth of the metaphysical problem. How can the ultimate reality be one movement? How can one movement give rise to infinite diversity? How can dead matter be the same movement as life? I can only indicate the nature of the argument, and try to give a picture of the way in which the ultimate reality is conceived. The argument is that the inversion of a movement may be brought about by simple interruption of the movement, and that if a movement, such as the creative act of will, a movement concentrated on a purpose, be conceived as a tension, its interruption in whatever way brought about is a detension. The word *detension*, the meaning of which is clearly expressed in its form, is employed because we have no exact word in ordinary use equivalent to it. It is meant to express that extension is really the de-tension of a tension. Matter, extension in space, is the interruption which is an inversion of the movement which in life is a pure duration in time. An illustration may show what is meant. If I am listening to a poet reciting his poem, my attitude of attention enables me to enter into the poet's meaning, his real creation. Let me, however, only relax my attention; all that I then have is the form of his expression, which may become for me words or sounds or even the pictures of the letters that compose the words. Or again, if I am bent on some purpose, my whole self seems gathered up into one point; let me relax a moment, and my self is scattered into memories, dreams, wandering thoughts. And more than this, the very dispersion may act as an opposing movement thwarting my purpose. It is in this way that the genesis of matter may be said to be involved in the very nature of the movement of life. It is indeed in this way that science tends to represent matter. It is a descending movement, a dispersion, a degradation of energy, and life in contrast is an

ascending or at least arresting or retarding movement. Vital activity is a reality making itself in a
reality which is unmaking itself.

Creation is not a mystery, for we experience it in
ourselves. We are confined to a very limited outlook; our actual experience of life is narrowed to
the view we may obtain of what it is and what it
has effected on the surface of this small planet.
But just as all that we know of other planets and
other solar systems seems to lead us to the conclusion
that they do not differ essentially from our own, so
we may conclude that the principle of reality is
everywhere the same. This principle is life or consciousness which is manifested in a need of creation.
If we would call that ultimate reality, the universal
principle underlying worlds and systems of worlds,
God, then we must say that God is unceasing life,
action, freedom. And creation is a simple process,
" an action that is making itself across an action
that is unmaking itself, like the fiery path of a rocket
through the black cinders of spent rockets that are
falling dead."

Can we say then what evolution means ? Does it
reveal to us the purpose and destiny of humanity ?
Only so far as this, it shows us that in one very
special sense we are the end and purpose of evolution. Not that we existed beforehand as its purpose
or final cause, for there is no pre-existent plan; the
impetus lies behind us, not before. Not that we are
the successful outcome of the impetus, the end of
its striving, for we are only the result of one divergent
tendency, and doubtless many accidents have helped

to determine the position in which we stand. But whereas everywhere else the current of life has been turned back by weight of the dead matter that confronted it, in man it has won free way. If we picture this impetus of life as a need of creation, an effort to achieve freedom, met by matter which is the opposite direction of its own movement, and which stands to it as necessity to freedom, if we see in the struggle the striving of life to introduce into matter the largest possible amount of freedom, then it is in man alone, capable of free creative action, that success has been attained. But the success has not been attained without sacrifice, and the success is very limited. It is only one form of conscious activity that has reached in us a full development. We are pre-eminently intellectual. A different evolution might have led to a more intuitive consciousness, or even to a full development of intellect and intuition in a more perfect humanity. In us intuition is almost completely sacrificed to intellect, but it is this intuition that philosophy seizes in order to reveal to us the unity of the spiritual life, the life that is wider than the intellect and the materiality to which it binds us. Philosophy shows us the life of the body on the road to the life of the spirit. " Life as a whole, from the initial impulsion that thrusts it into the world, appears as a wave which rises, and which is opposed by the descending movement of matter. On the greater part of its surface, at different heights, the current is converted by matter into a vortex. At one point alone it passes freely, dragging with it the obstacle which will weigh on its progress but will not stop it. At that point is humanity ; it is our privileged situation." Shall we always drag the obstacle ? Perhaps not. Humanity may be able to beat down every resistance and overcome even death.

Thus philosophy introduces us into the spiritual life. It shows us in the intuition of our own personal life the true duration in which memory and will form one free acting present. It shows us the exact point at which matter exists, that sharp cutting point at which the past is entering the future, a point which in abstraction from memory and will has no existence. By sympathetic insight we realise that our duration is one with the whole reality of the universe, vast as we conceive it to be. We see that if the universe is real it can only mean that it lives as a consciousness which endures and becomes unceasingly. That for this universal life as for every individual life, matter is the momentary point without duration that exists only where the movement is creating. And so the whole seeming deadweight of matter is a view only of universal life. It is nothing to us therefore that the life which has evolved on this planet is small and weak compared to the mass of the dead matter it has moved within ; that it is confined to the surface, and that the energy it has arrested is derived from the sun ; for the life that is manifest in this creative evolution is one in principle with universal life. The descending movement may be here more powerful than the ascending movement, so that life on this planet may be only arresting a descent. In other worlds it may be otherwise, for even in the universe that science reveals worlds are being born.

Why is it then that the appearance is so different to the reality ? Why is this view of the ceaseless living, the continual becoming, the free creating activity so difficult to realise, so counter to all our habits of thought, so contrary to what daily experience seems to teach ? Why, if this philosophy reveals simple truth, is it only at rare moments and by difficult abstraction that we are able to realise it, and then only in passing glimpses ? Why at ordinary times does it seem so certain that it is material things that endure, and that time is a mechanical play of things that themselves do not change ? It is due to two illusions of the human mind. They are fundamental illusions, for they bring to us so essential an advantage in the practical direction of our activity that without them we should be different beings from what we are. In our practical life we only observe in movement the thing that moves, in becoming the different states, in duration the succeeding instants ; and this is necessary for our action ; but it leads to an illusion when we try to think what real movement, real becoming, and real duration are, for it leads us to suppose that we are thinking of movement when we are in fact thinking of states which neither move nor change. This is the first illusion, that we can think the moving by means of the immobile. The second illusion is that we think that there is a real unreality. In all our action we aim at getting something we feel we want, at creating something that does not exist, and so we represent this need as a void, this not yet existing something as an absence, an unreality, nothing. There is no unreality, no nothing. It is an illusion to imagine that we can pass out of reality. Unreality, nothing, means not the absolute non-existence of everything, but the absence of the reality we want by reason of the presence of a reality that does not interest us.

Philosophy reveals to us a reality that is consistent with the satisfaction of our highest ideals. It discloses the life of the spirit. It may give us neither God nor immortality in the old theological meaning of those terms, and it does not show us human life and individual conduct as the chief end, purpose, and centre of interest of the universe. But the reality of life is essentially freedom. Philosophy delivers us from the crushing feeling of necessity that the scientific conception of a closed mechanical universe has imposed on modern thought. Life is a free activity in an open universe. We may be of little account in the great whole. Humanity itself and the planet on which it has won its success may be an infinitesimal part of the universal life, but it is one and identical with that life, and our struggle and striving is the impetus of life. And this above all our spiritual life means to us, the past has not perished, the future is being made.

BIBLIOGRAPHY

Time and Freewill: An Essay on the Immediate Data of Consciousness. Swan Sonnenschein & Co., 1910.
    The translation by F. L. Pogson of the *Essai sur les données immédiates de la conscience.* Paris, 1888.

Matter and Memory: Swan Sonnenschein & Co., 1911.
    The translation by N. M. Paul and W. S. Palmer of *Matière et Mémoire, Essai sur la relation du corps avec l'esprit.* Paris, 1896.

Creative Evolution. Macmillan & Co. 1911.
    The translation by Arthur Mitchell of *L'Évolution créatrice.* Paris, 1907.

Laughter: An Essay on the Meaning of the Comic. Macmillan & Co. 1911.
    The translation by C. Brereton and F. Rothwell of *Le Rire, Essai sur la signification du comique.* Paris, 1901.

La Perception du Changement: Conferences faites a l'Université d'Oxford les 26 et 27 Mai, 1911. Oxford: The Clarendon Press.

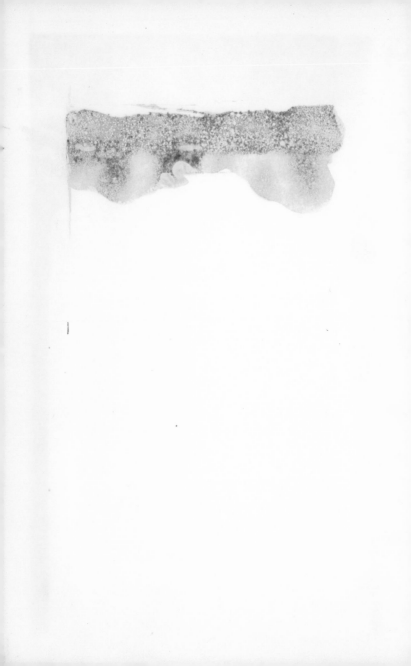

DATE DUE